BIRDS COLORING BOOK

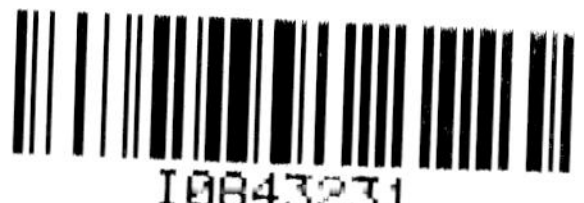

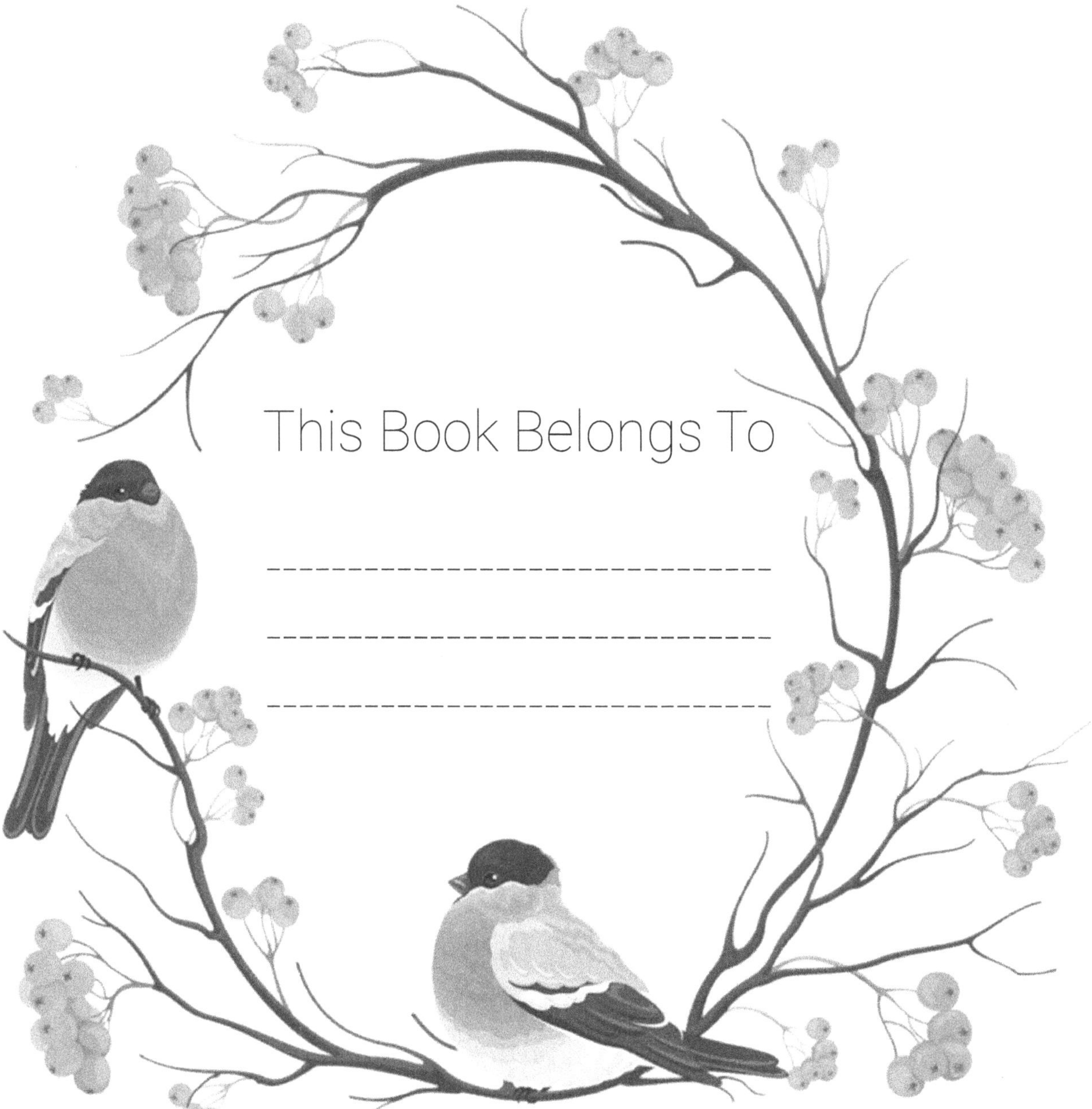

This Book Belongs To

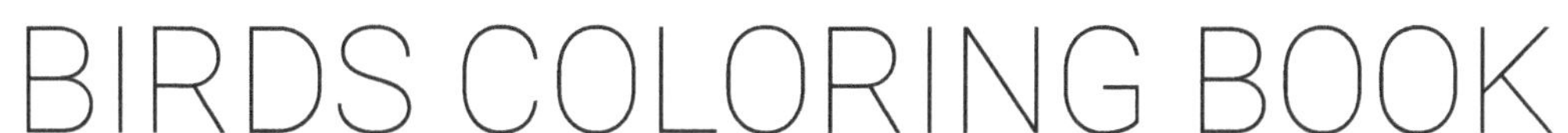

____

____

____

Copyright © 2019

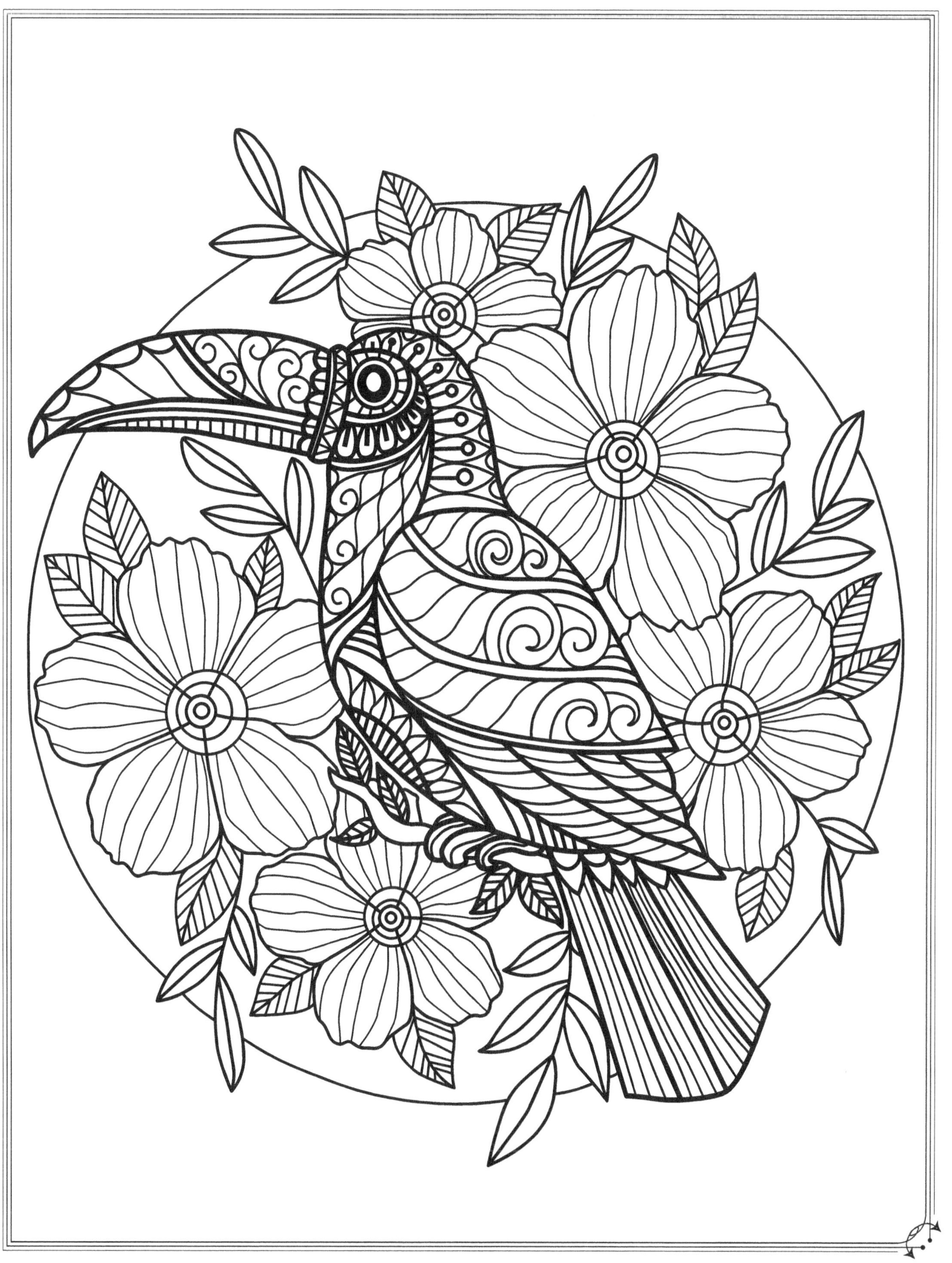

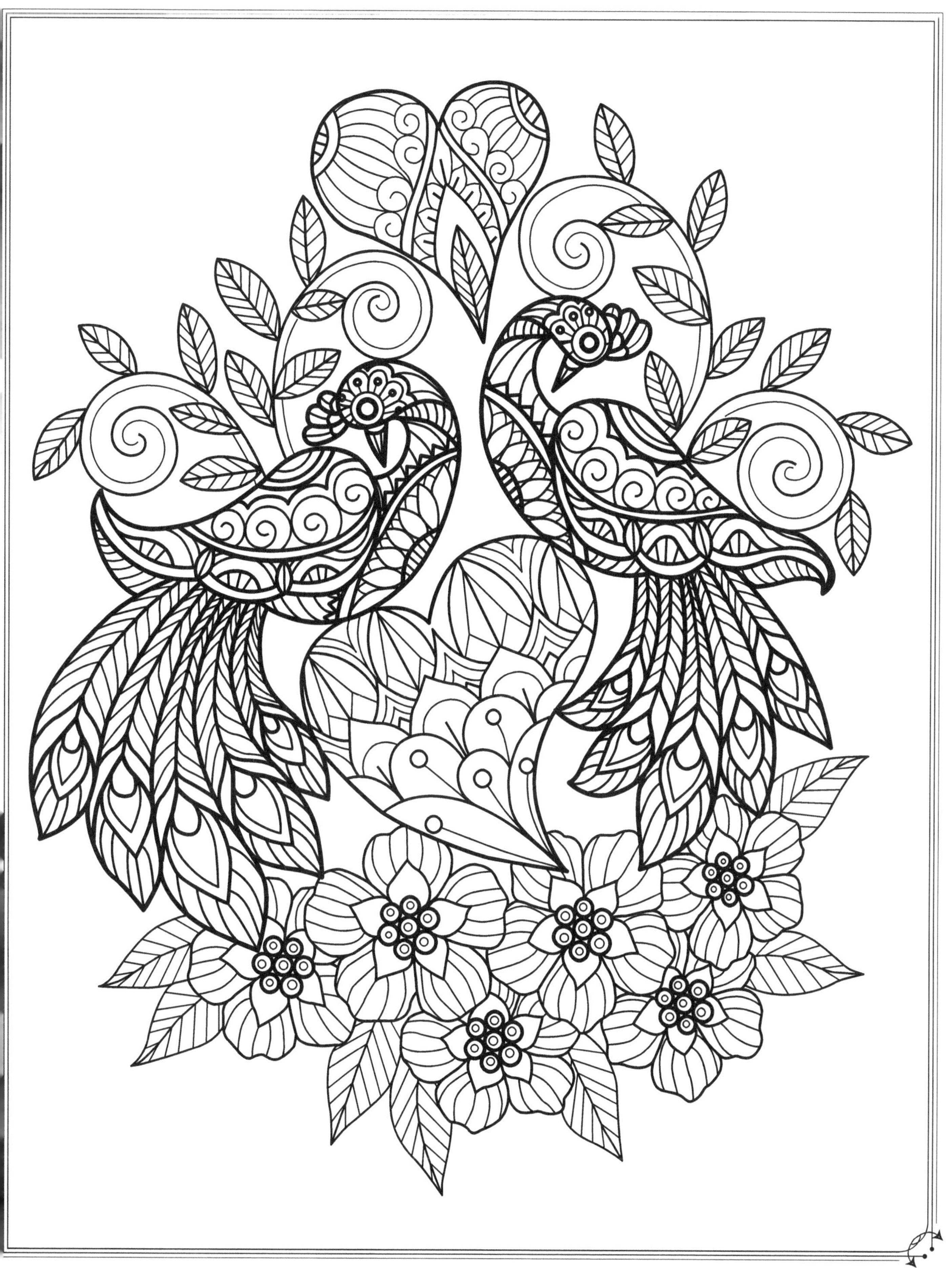

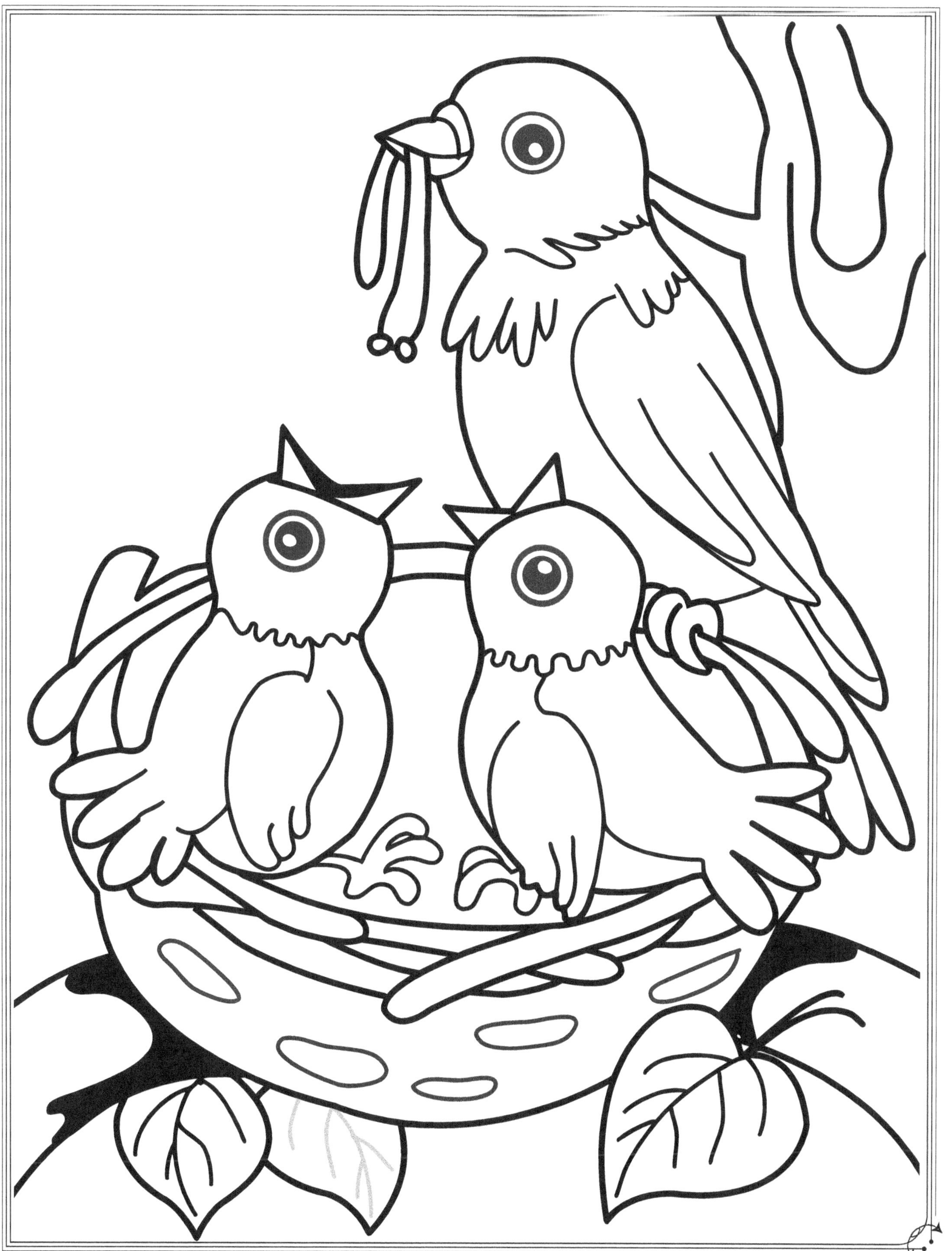

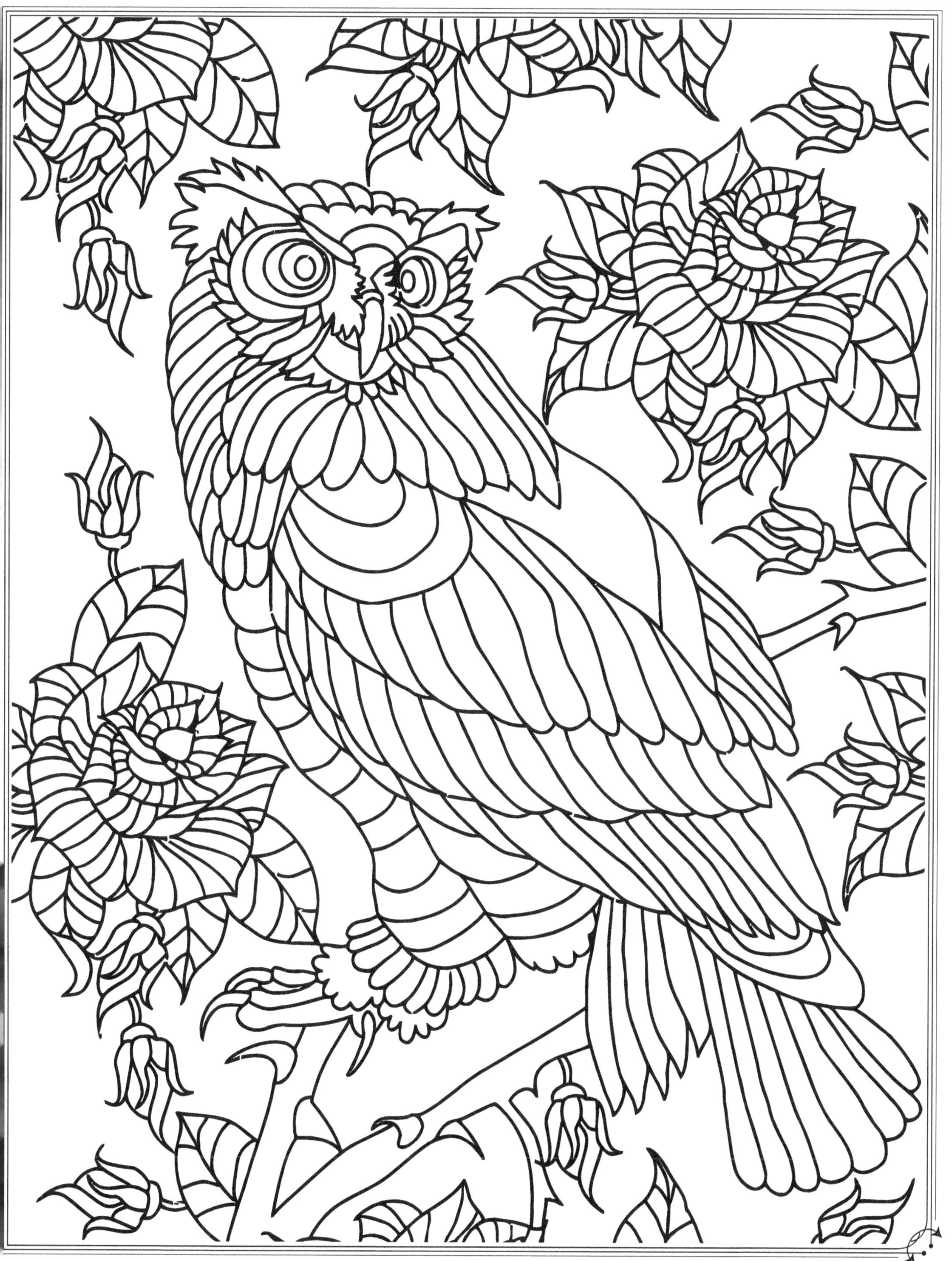

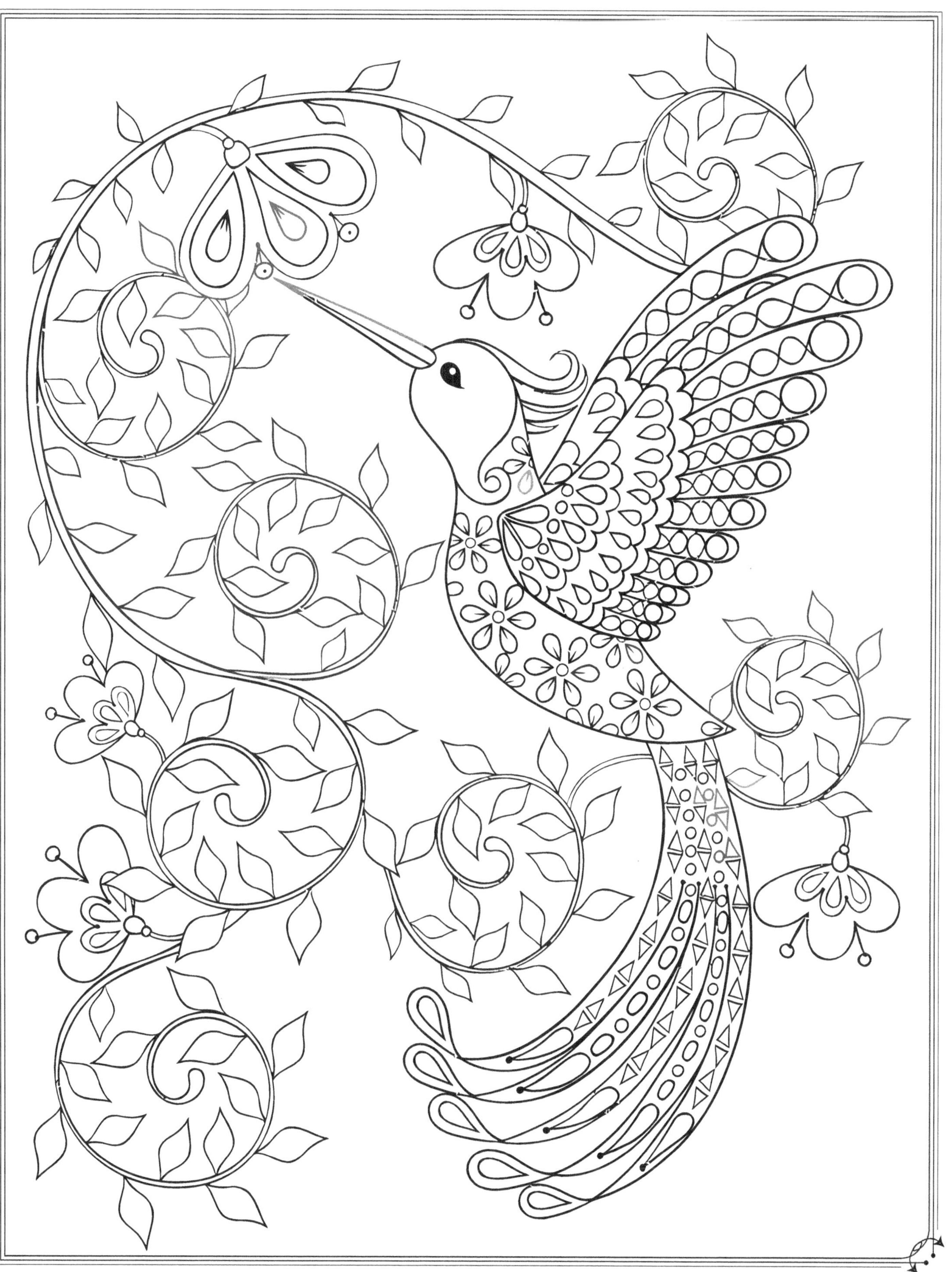

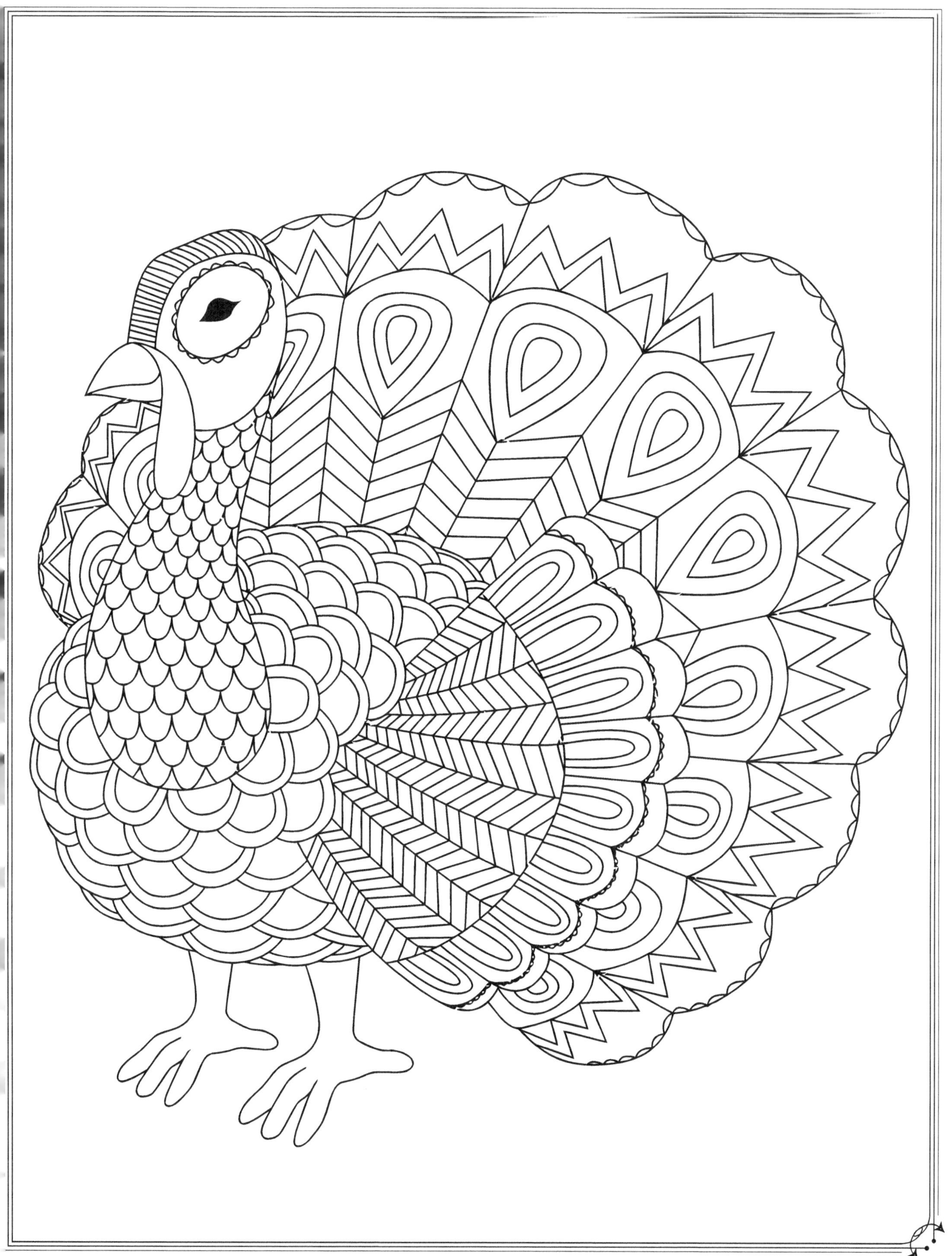

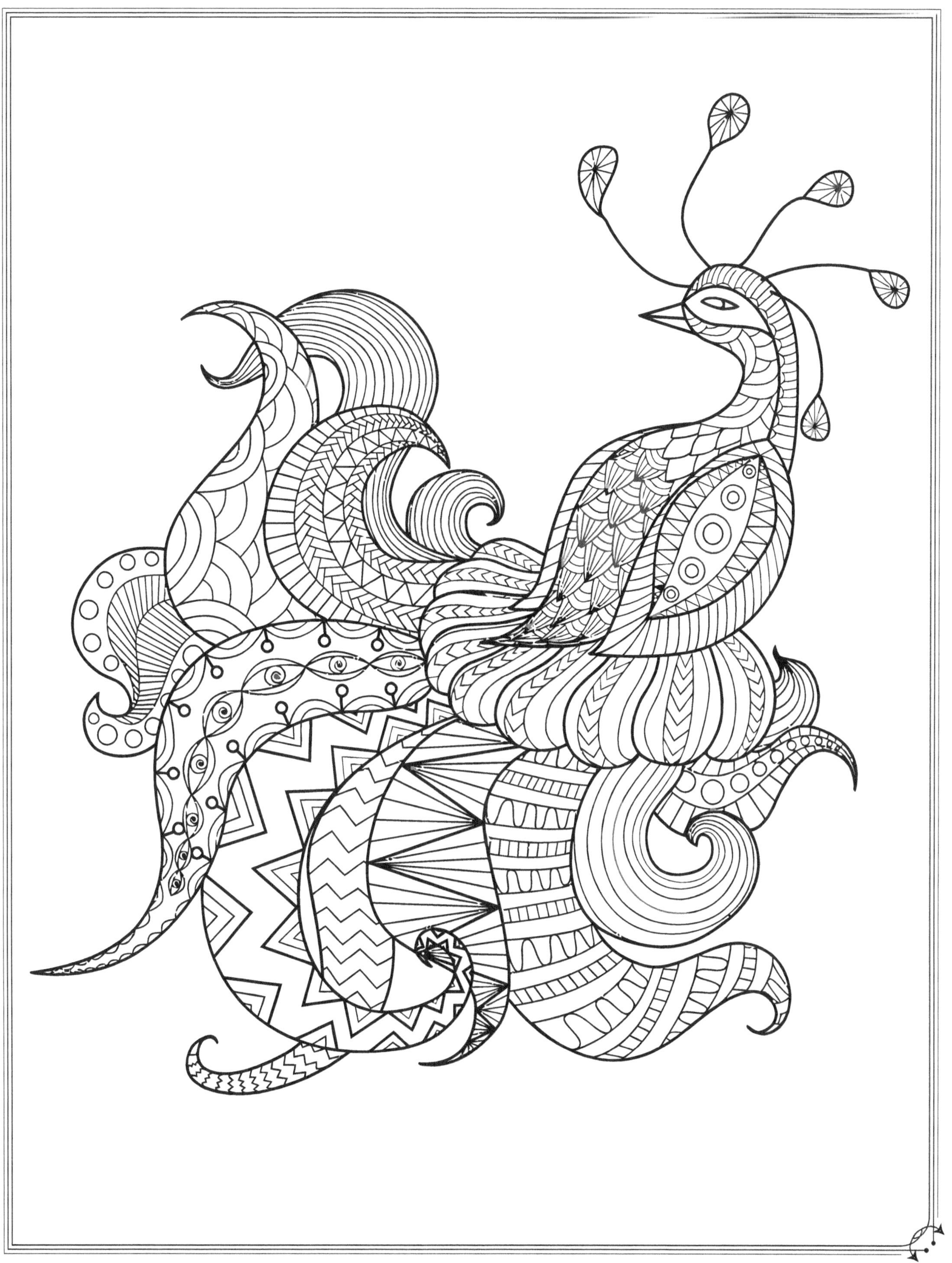

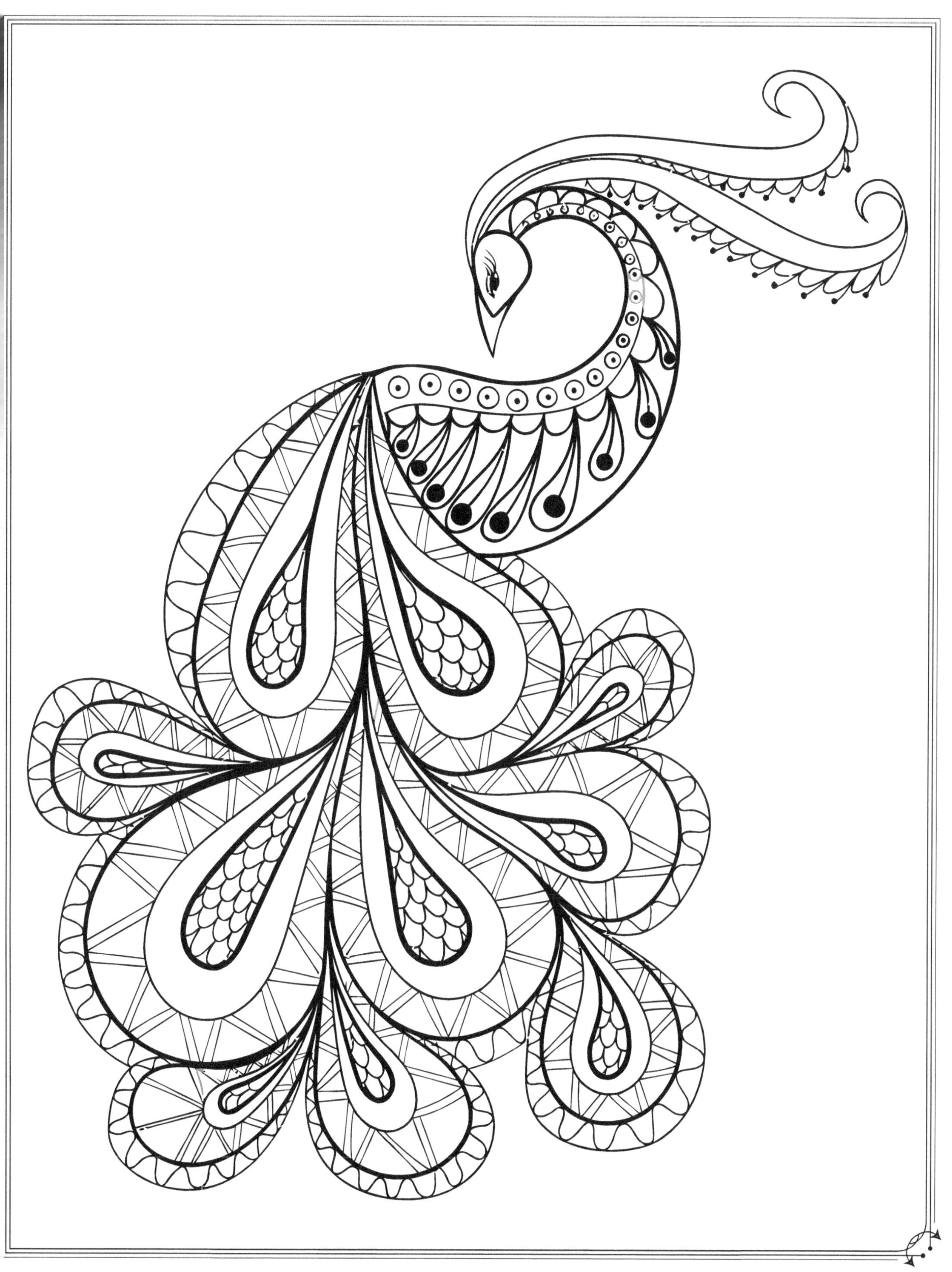

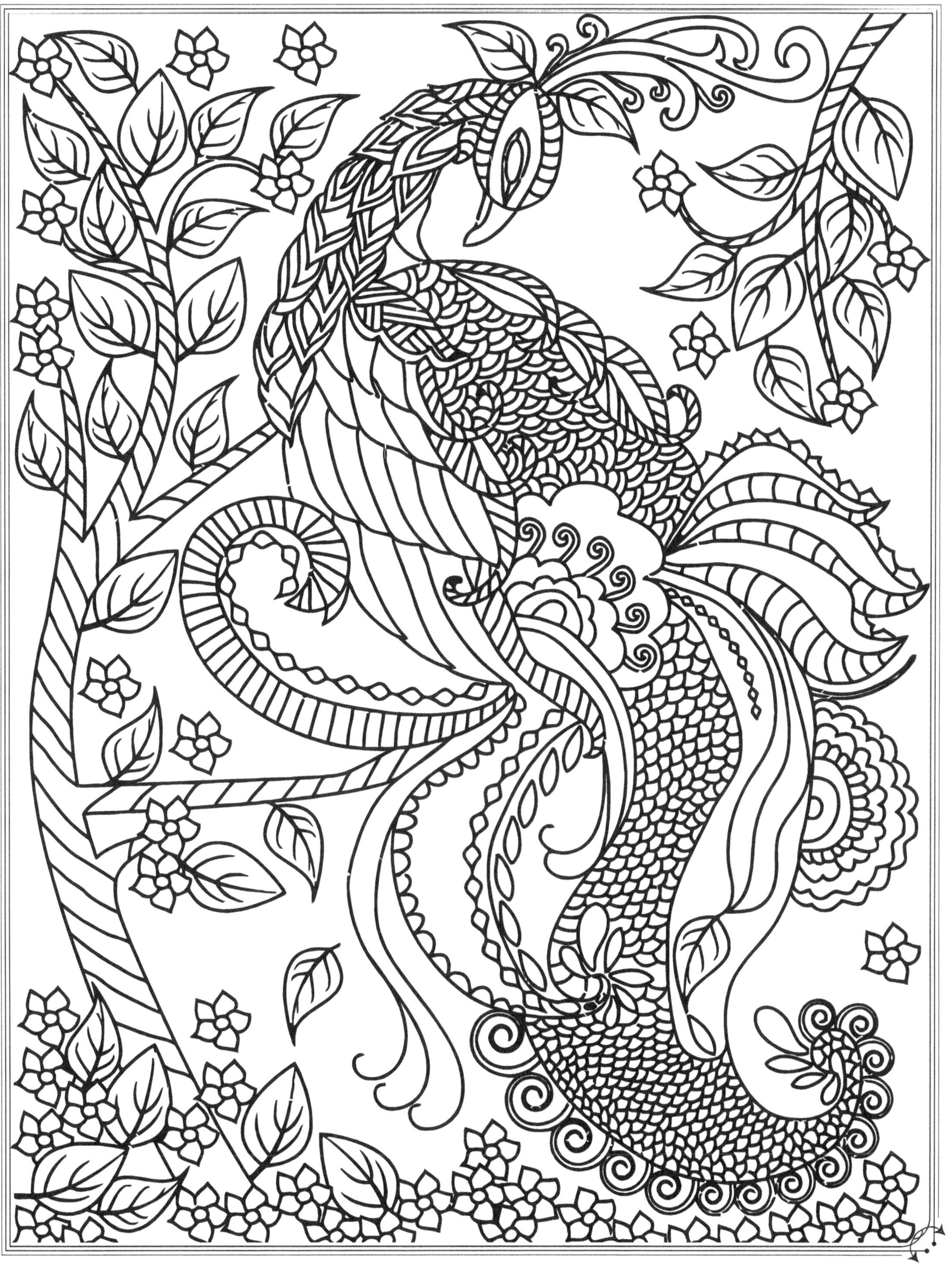

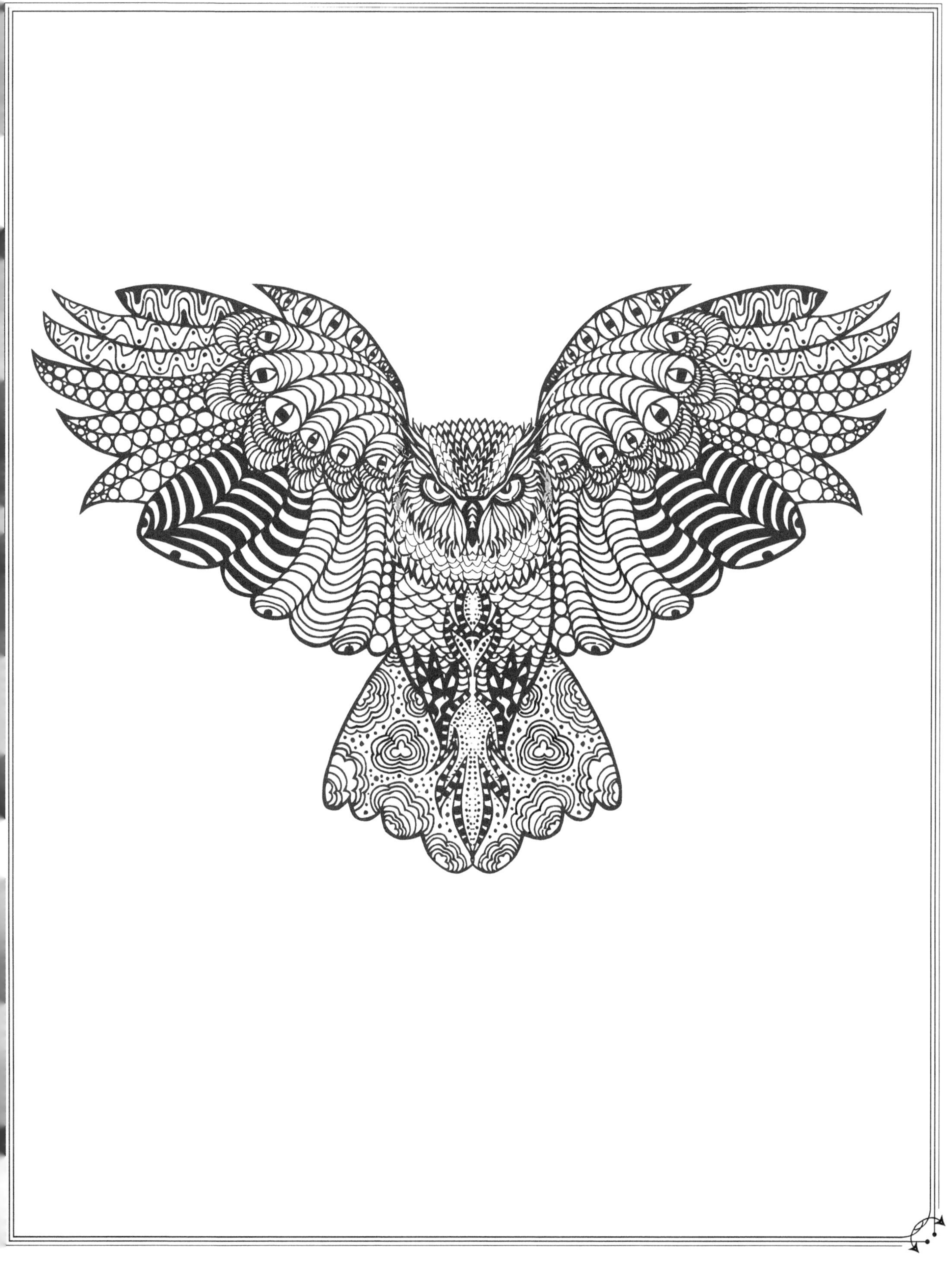

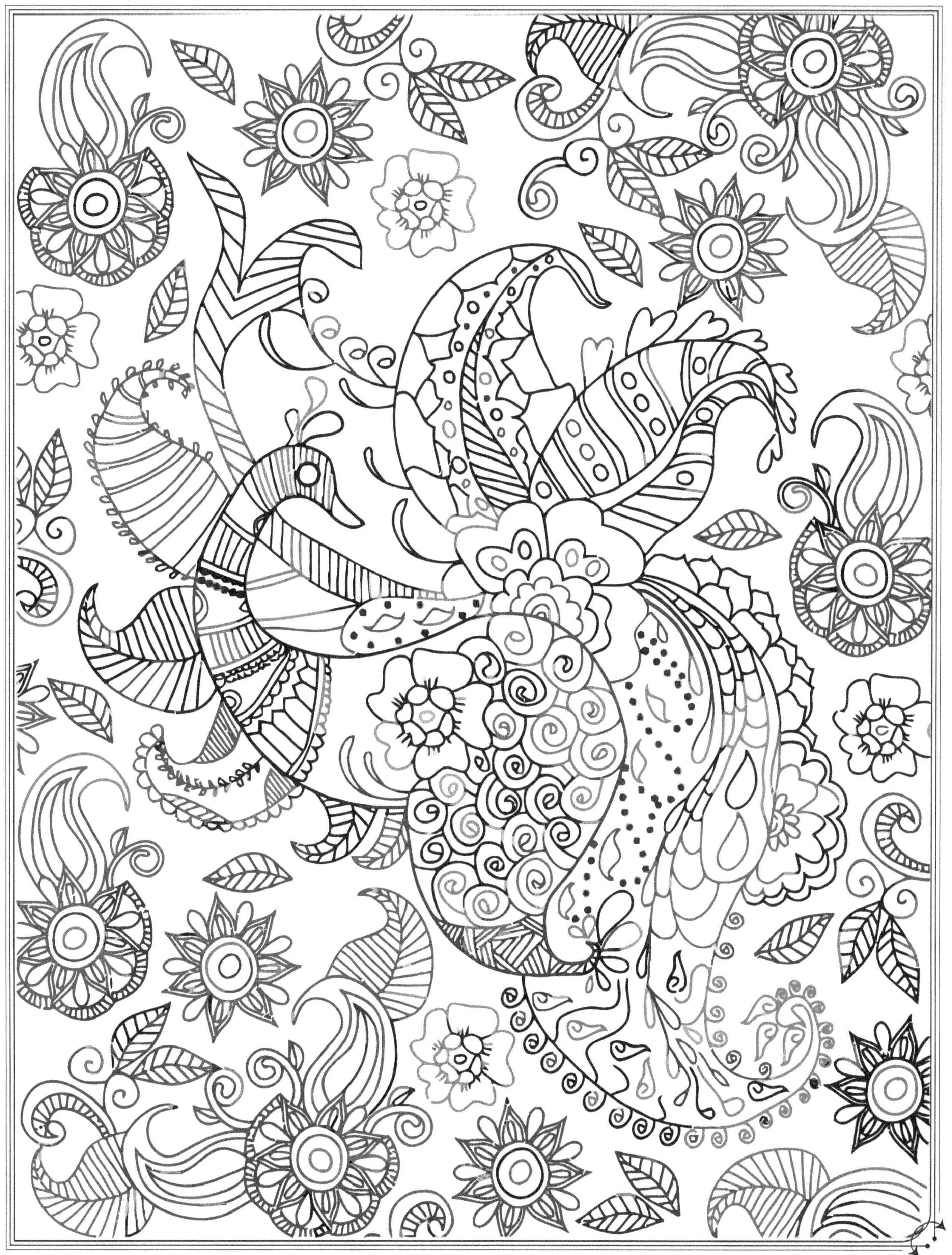

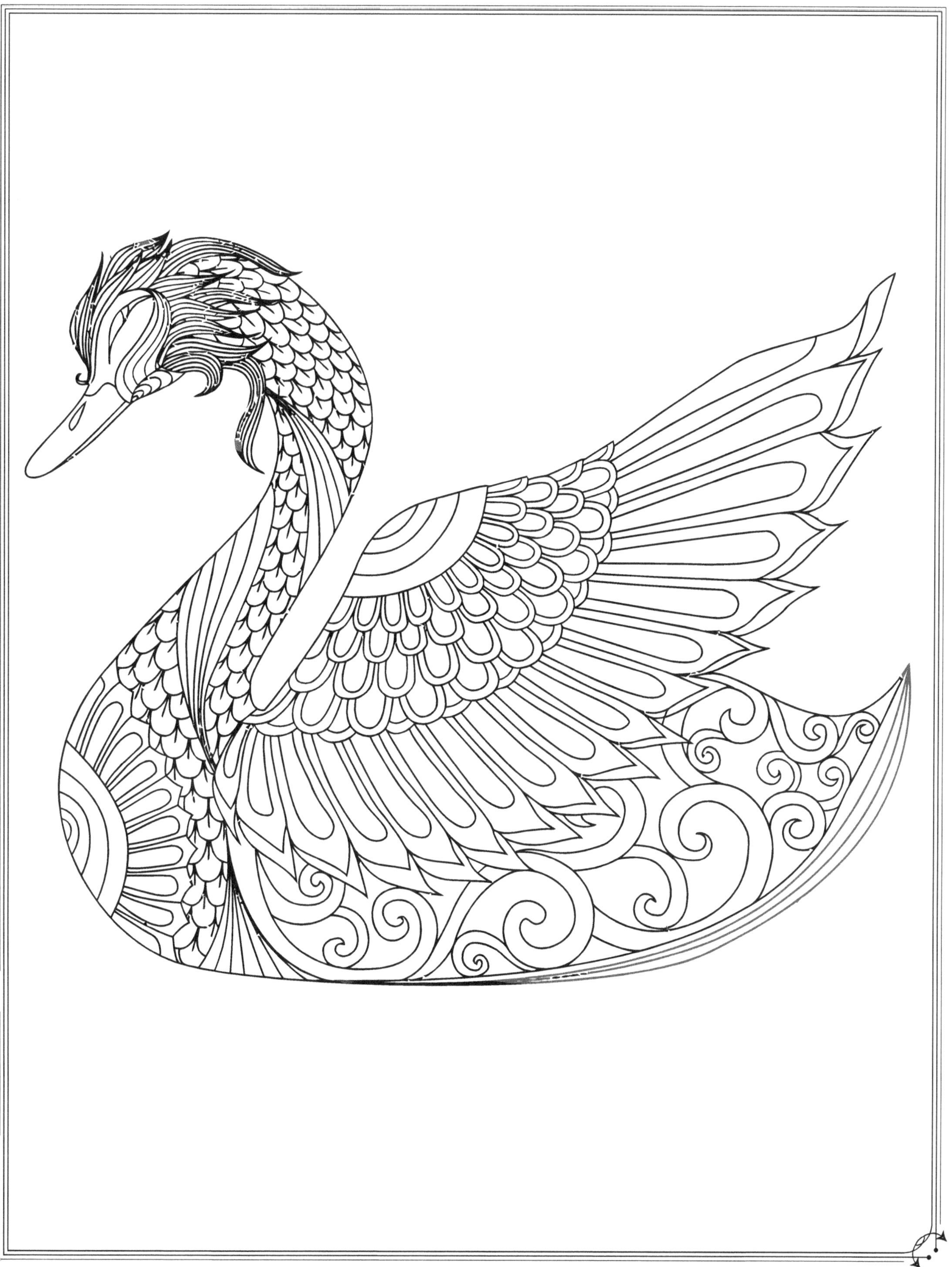

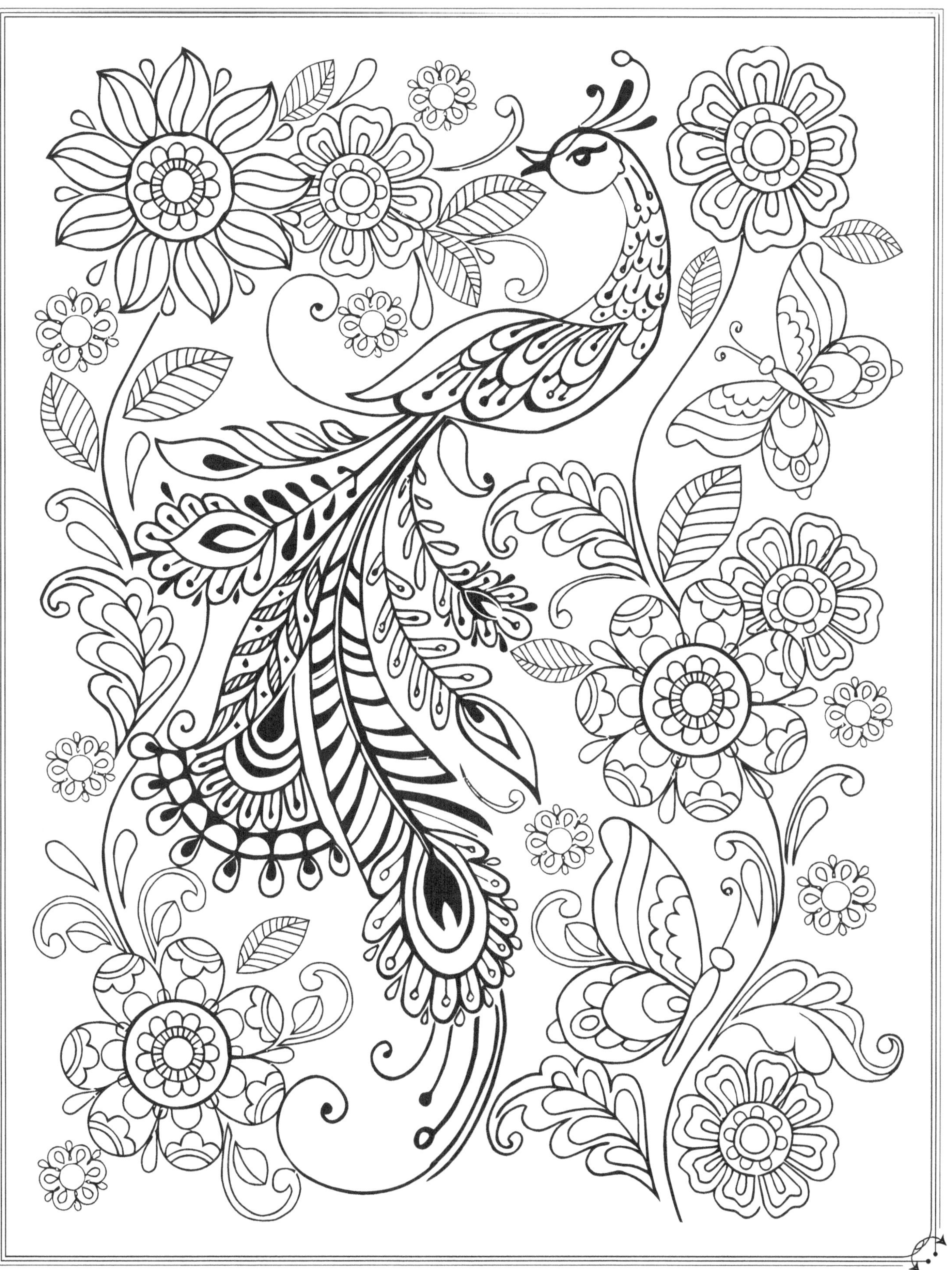

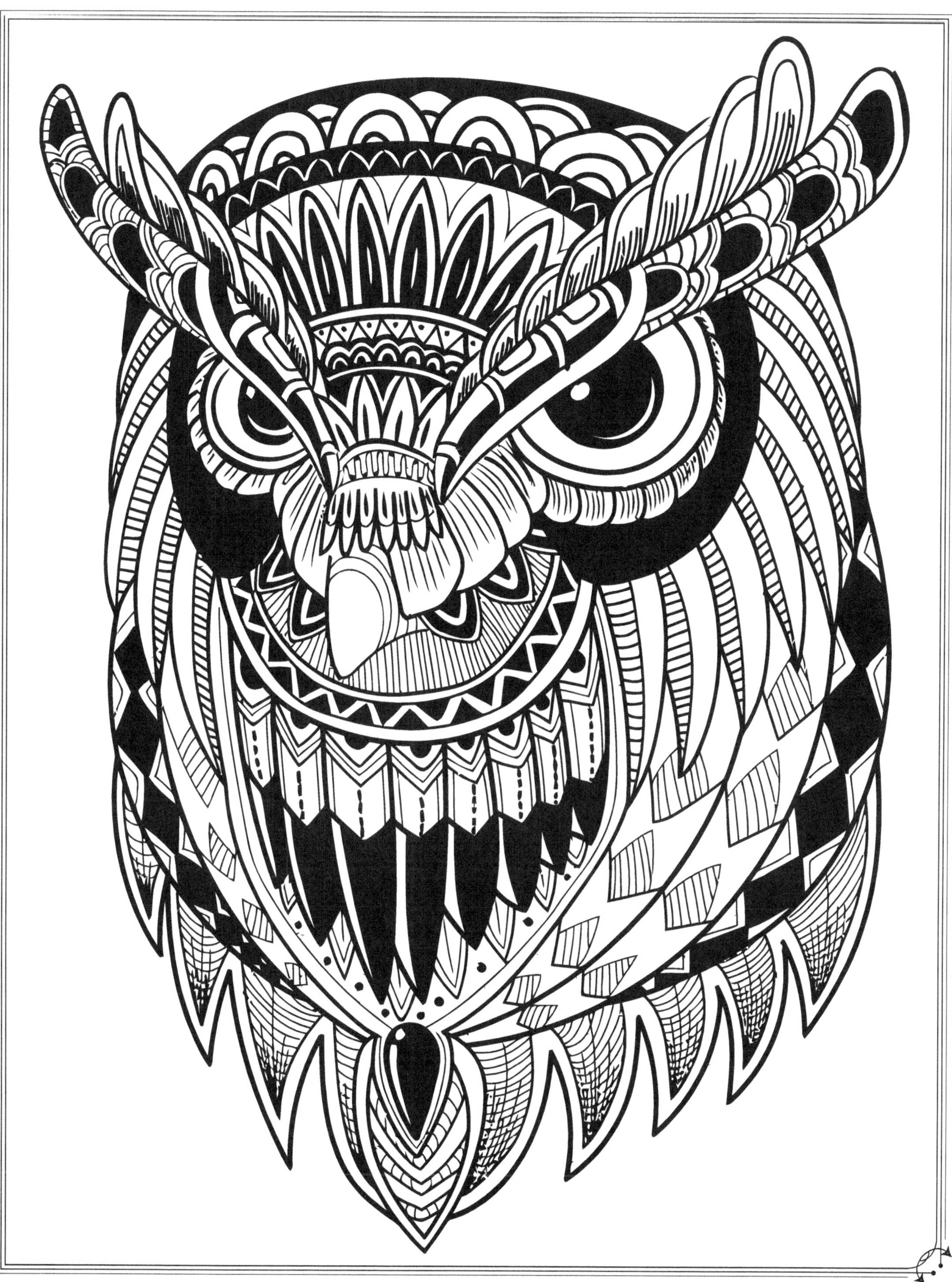

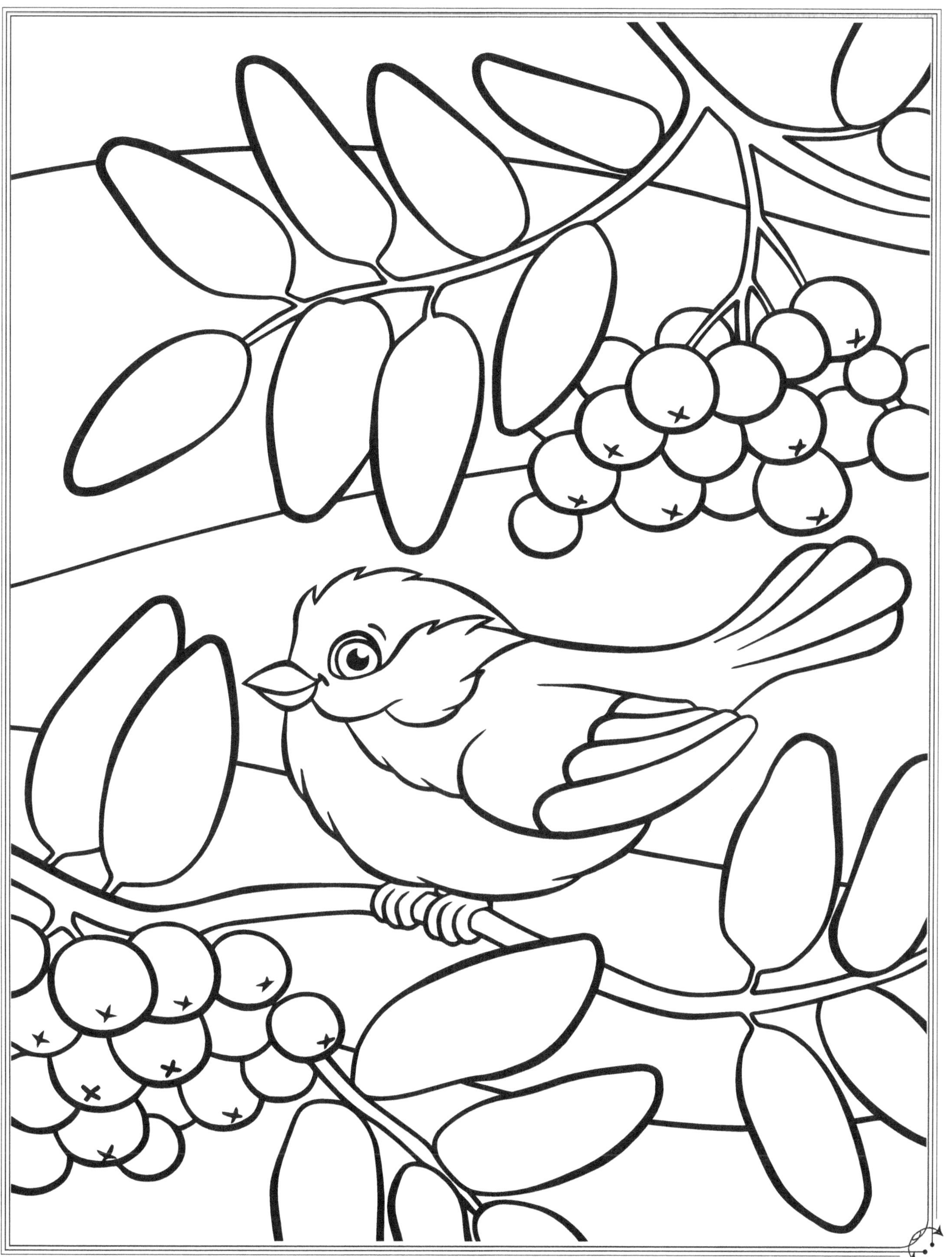

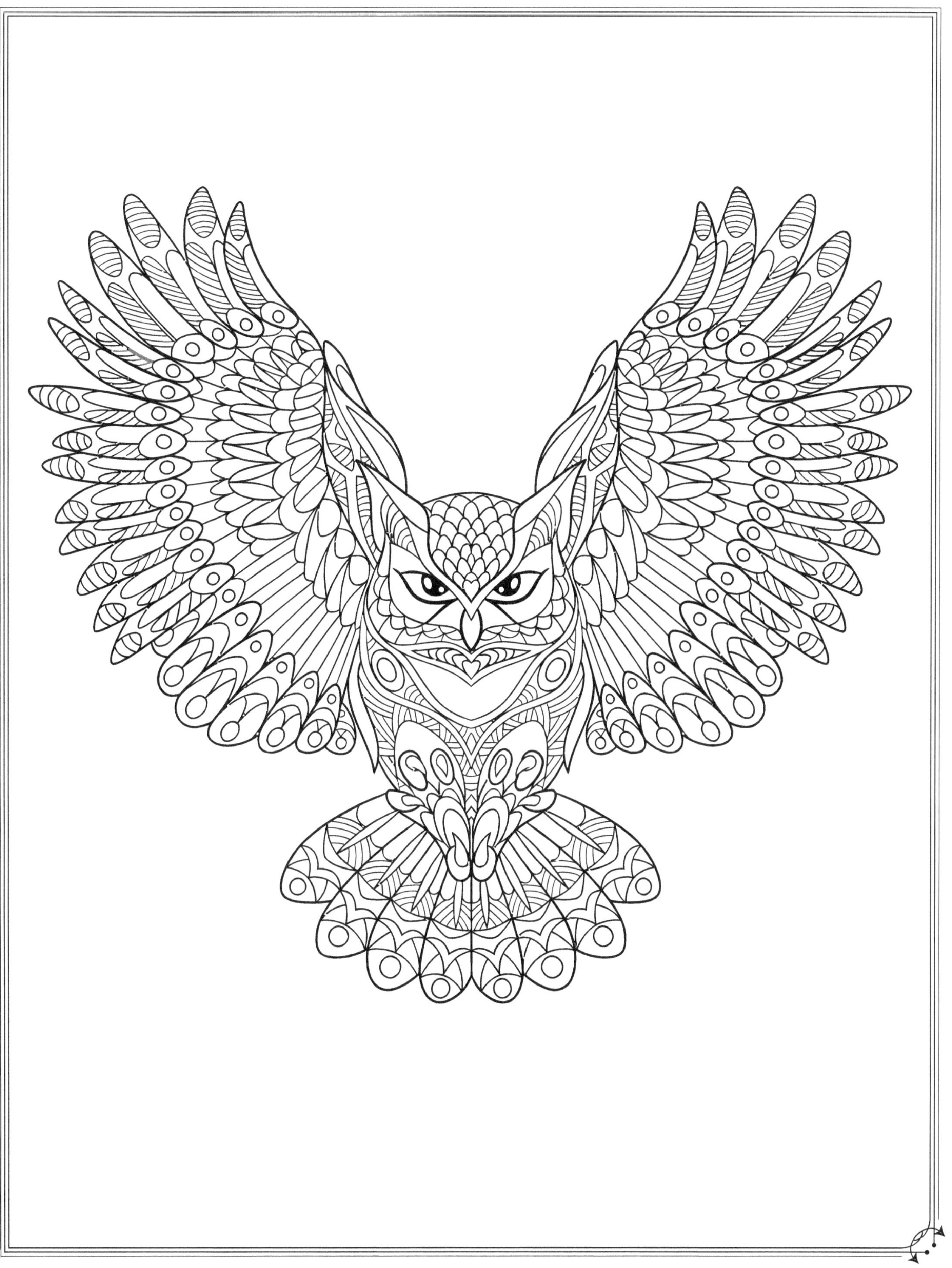

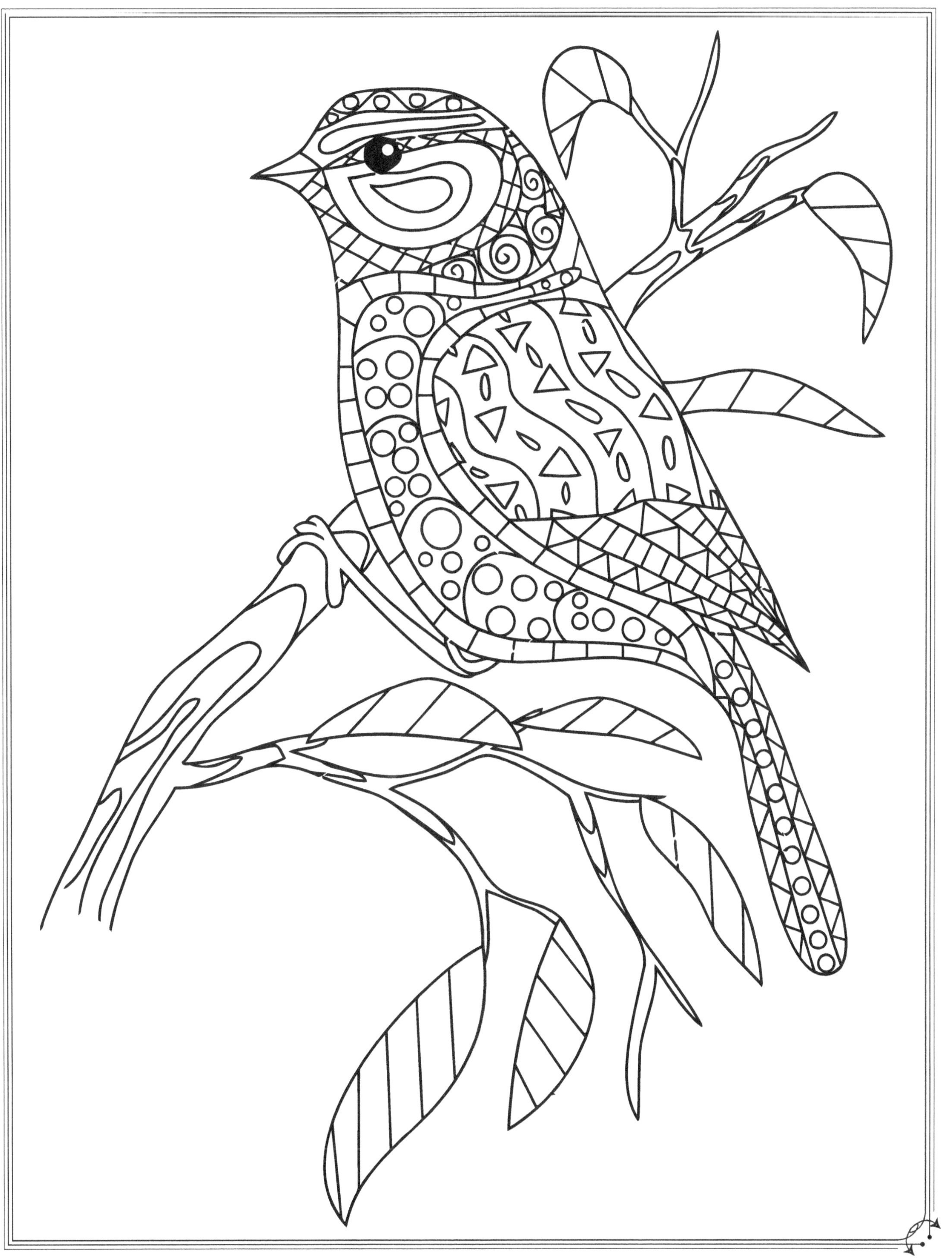

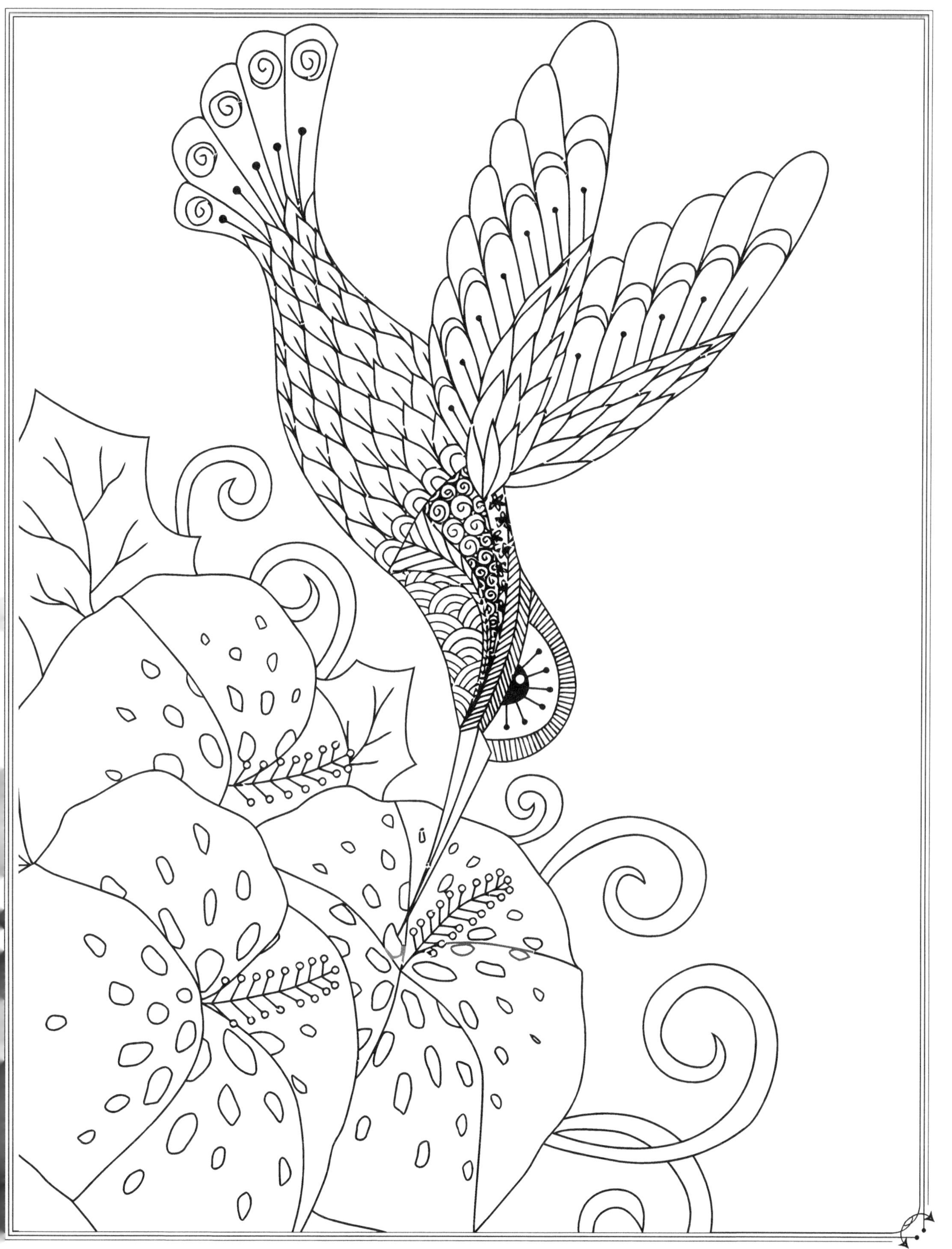

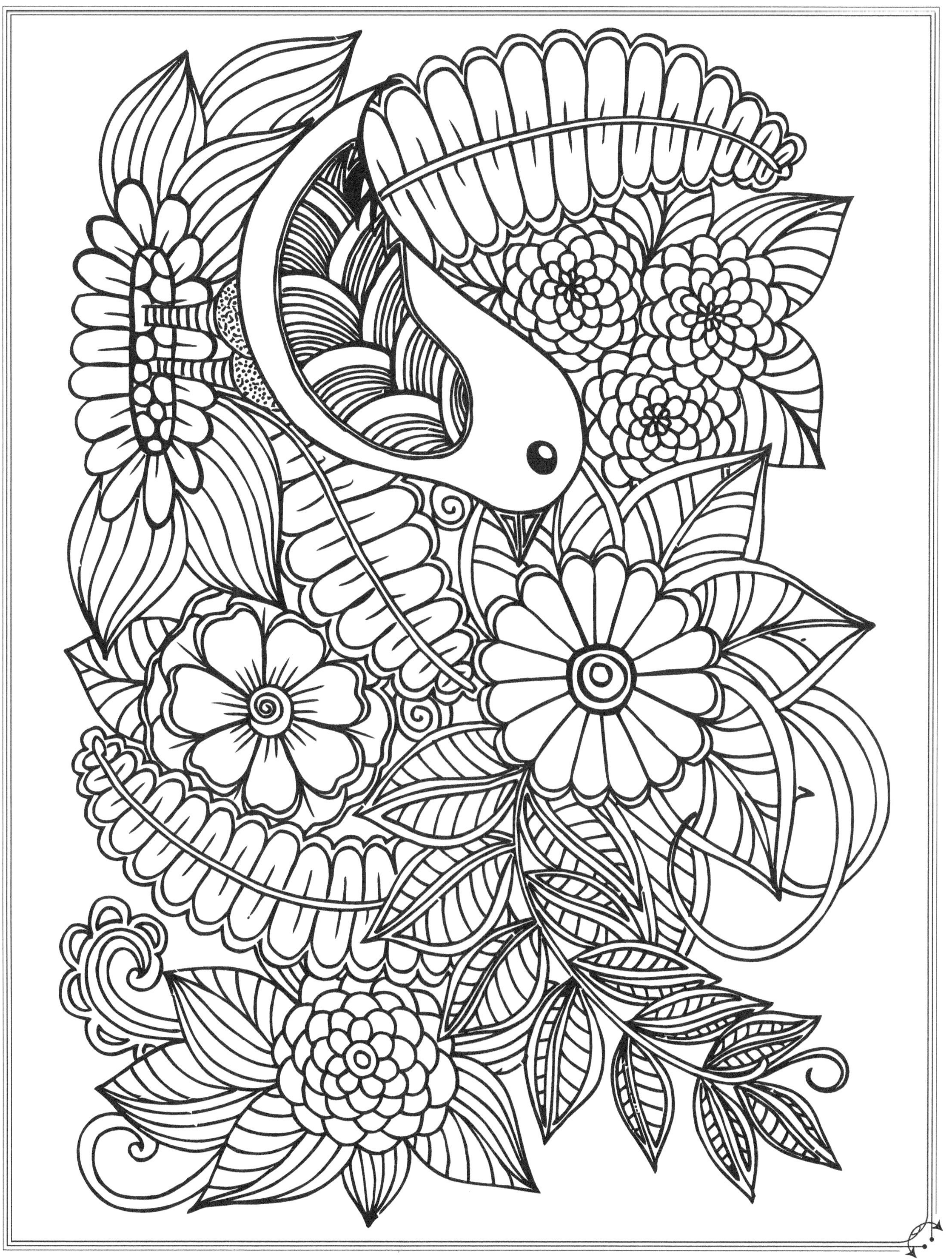

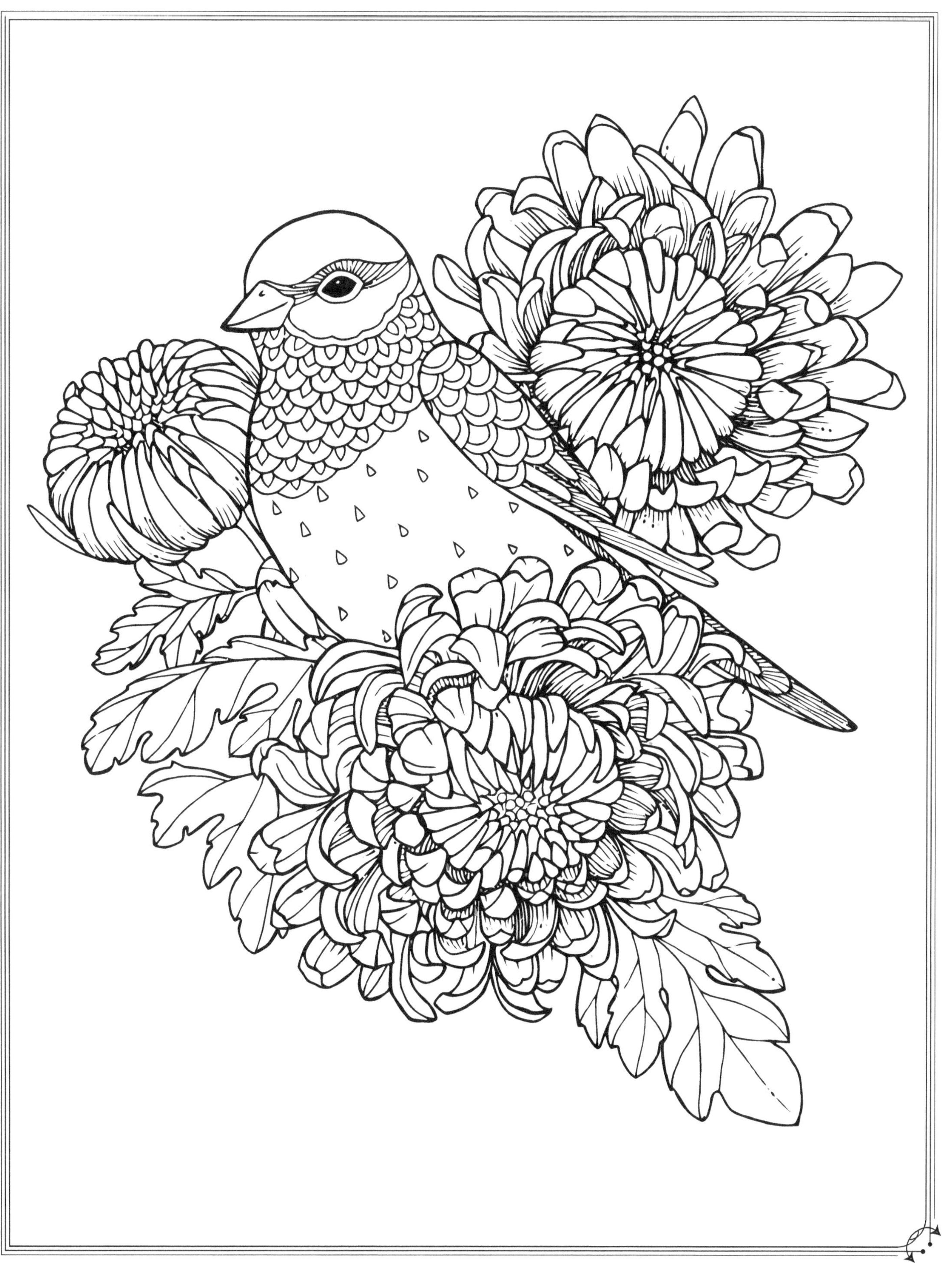

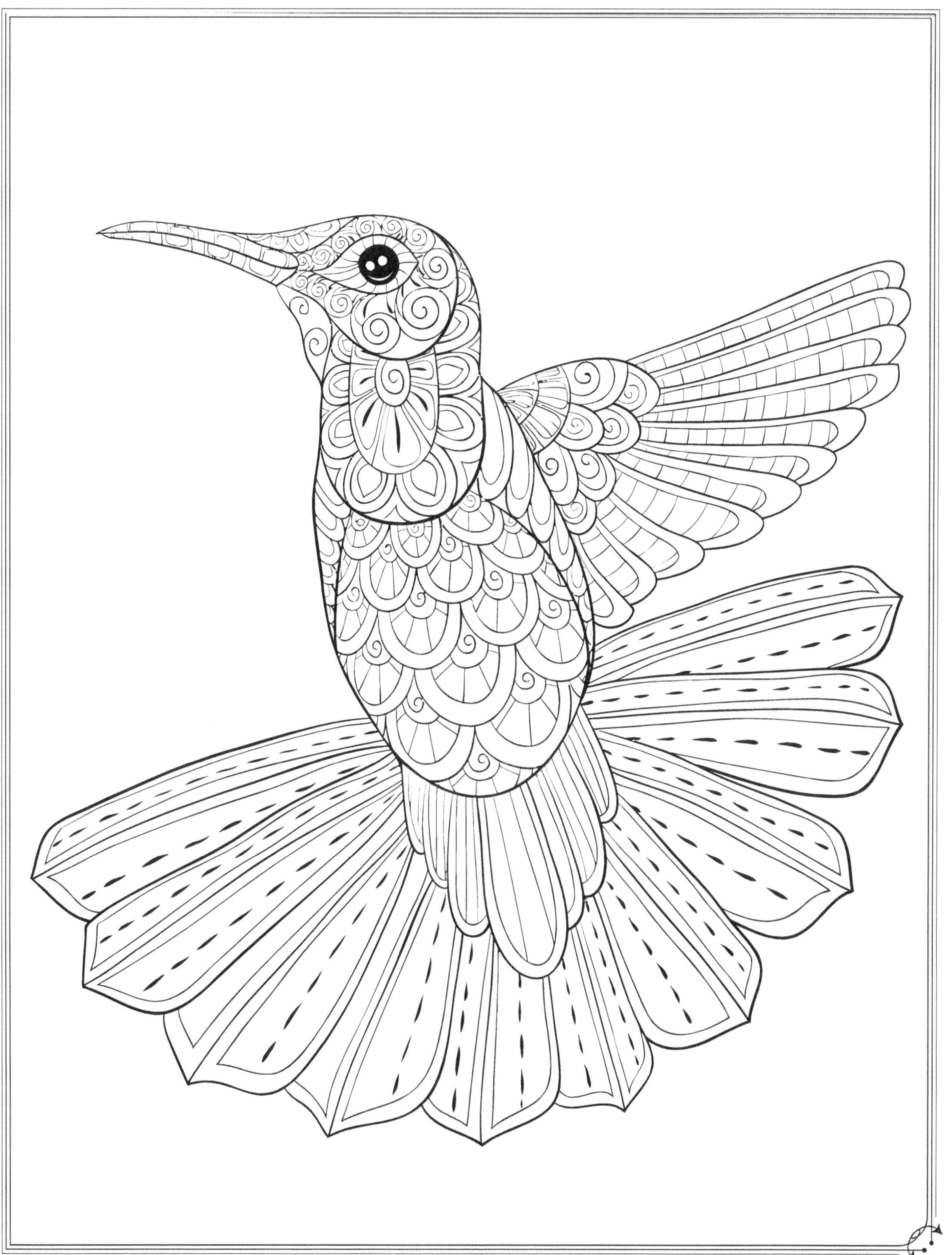

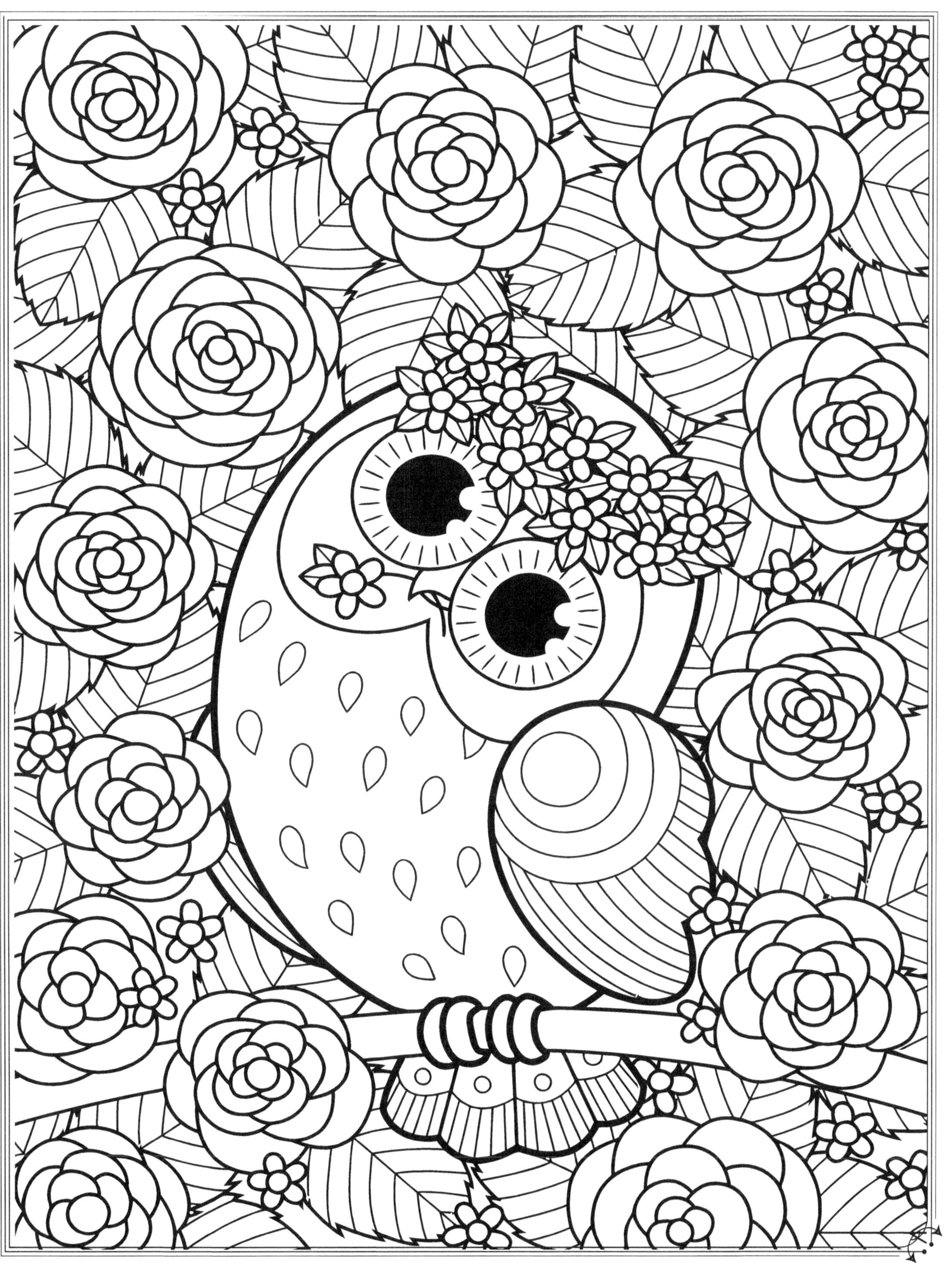

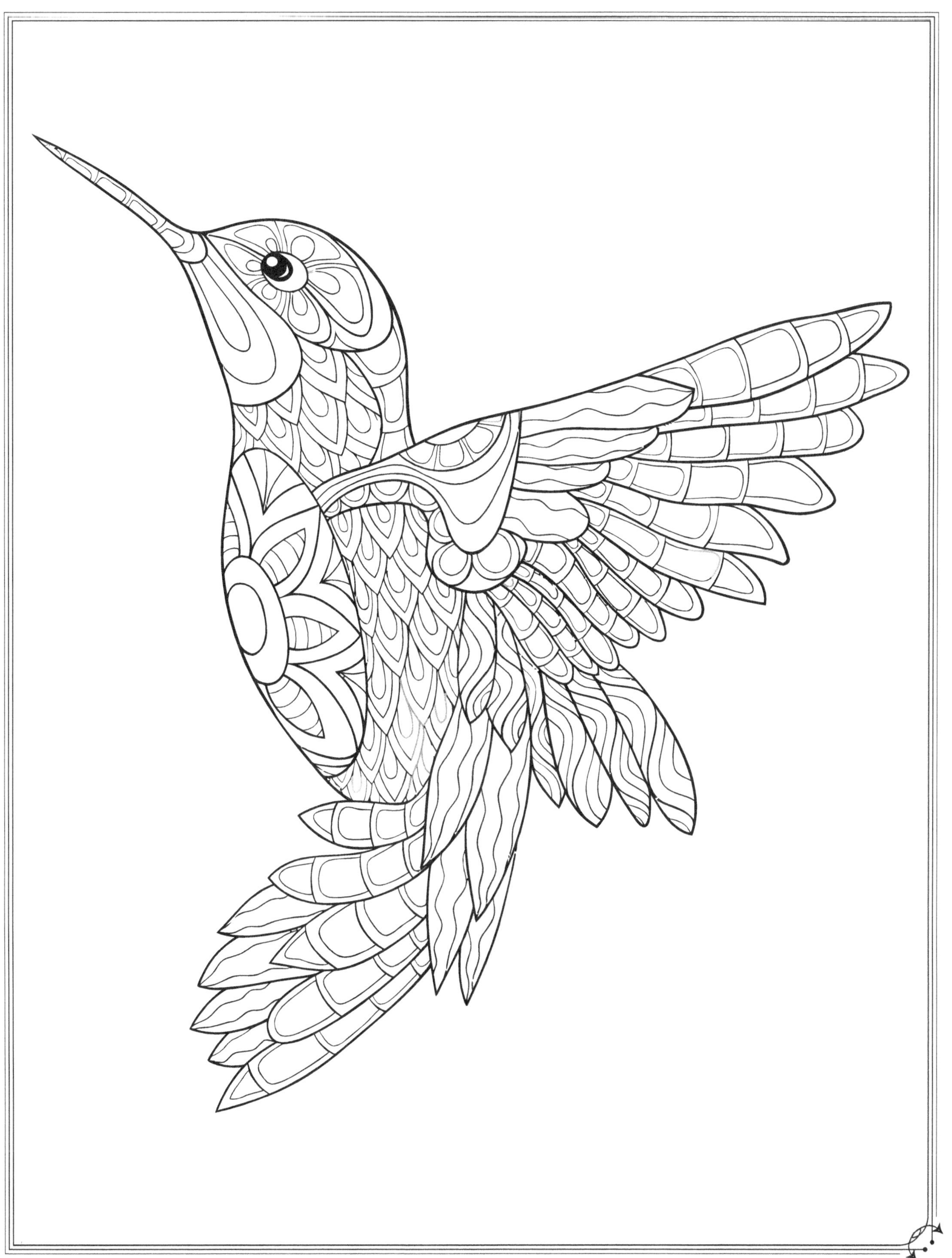

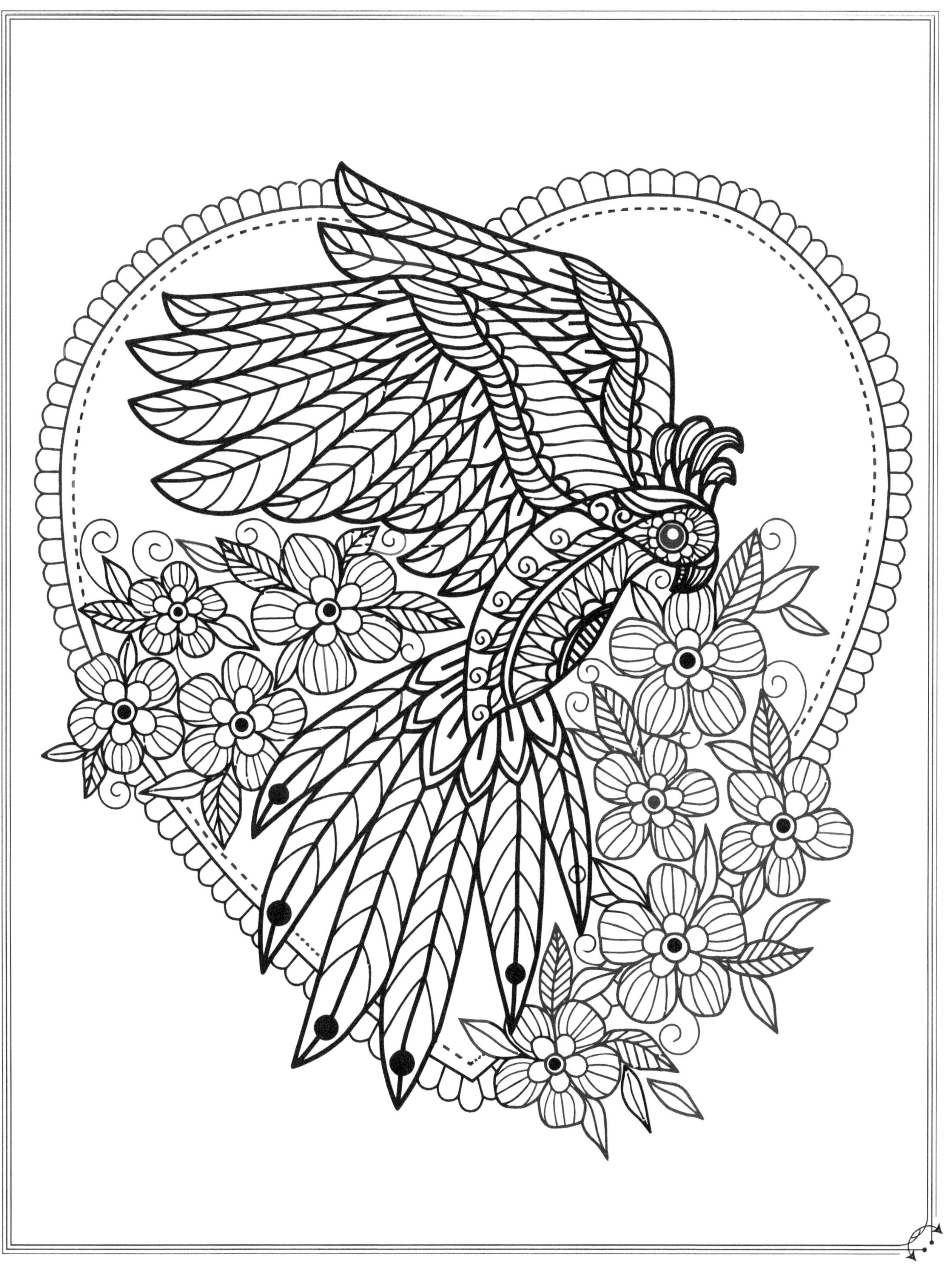